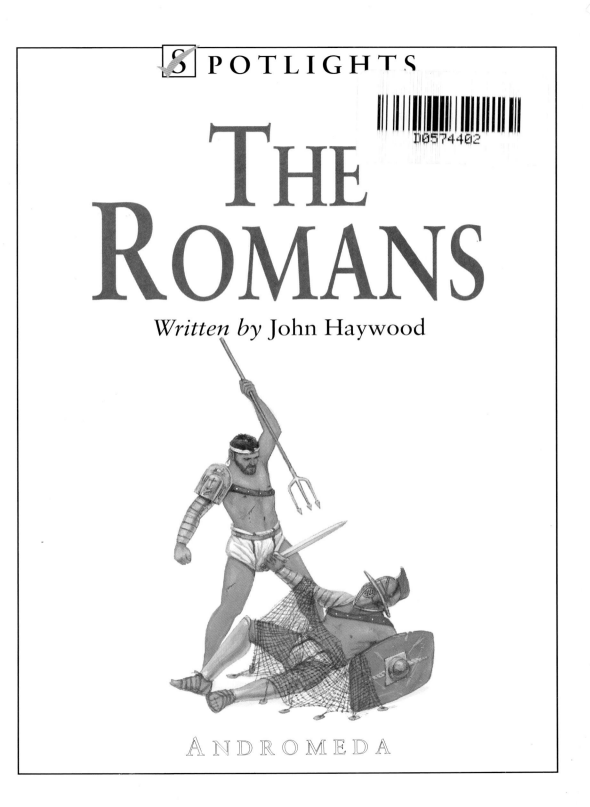

SPOTLIGHTS

THE ROMANS

Written by John Haywood

D0574402

ANDROMEDA

ACKNOWLEDGMENTS

Illustrated by
Julian Baker - Artists-Illustrators: 16-17, 26-27, 28-29
Bill Le Fever: Spotlights 8-43
Chris Forsey: 36
Kevin Maddison: 26 inset
Maltings Partnership: 8-9, 18-19, 20-21
Roger Payne - Linden Artists: 38-39, 42-43
Julia Pearson - Specs Art Agency: 30-31, 33 inset
Pete Roberts - Allied Artists: 10-11, 40-41
Tony Smith: 24-25, 32-33, 34-35, 37,
Mark Stacey - David Lewis Management: 12-13, 14-15
Mark Viney - Allied Artists: 22-23

Planned and produced by
Andromeda Oxford Limited
11-15 The Vineyard
Abingdon
Oxfordshire OX14 3PX

ISBN 1 871869 90 0

Printed in Singapore by Tien Wah Press

CONTENTS

INTRODUCTION

The Roman empire was one of the largest in world history. It was also one of the most successful, and it lasted for over 700 years. Even though their empire came to an end 1,500 years ago, the Romans still have an influence on our lives.

Our alphabet was invented by the Romans. The languages of modern France, Portugal, Spain, Italy and Romania are all descended from Latin, the Romans' language. The English language also contains thousands of Latin words. The laws of many countries, such as France and Germany, are based on Roman laws. Many of Europe's great cities, like London and Paris, were founded by the Romans. All over Europe, Roman buildings still stand to remind us of this great civilization.

VISITING MUSEUMS

All sorts of objects which the Romans used in their daily lives have survived to the present day. Many of them can be seen in museums all over the world. You can find similar examples to most of the objects illustrated in this book in a museum with a good Roman collection.

HOW TO USE THIS BOOK

This book explores and explains the world of the ancient Romans. Each double-page spread looks at a particular aspect of life in the Roman empire, building up a fascinating picture of this important civilization.

INTRODUCTION

Concise yet highly informative, this text introduces the reader to the topics covered in the spread. This broad coverage is complemented by more detailed exploration of particular points in the numerous captions.

INSET ARTWORKS

Subjects that help to explain particular points are shown in inset along with an explanation of their significance.

SPOTLIGHTS

A series of illustrations at the bottom of each page encourages the reader to look out for objects from ancient Rome that can be found in museums.

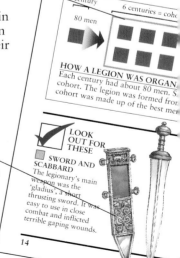

THE RO[M

The main reason [...] were able to conq[...] empire was their w[...] and highly trained [...] was an attractive ca[...] men. There was the [...] being killed but the w[...] good and, if they surv[...] soldiers enjoyed many [...] The main strength of t[...] was the legions of inf[...] recruited only from Ro[...] citizens. There were als[...] support troops called au[...]

century   6 centuries = coho[...]
80 men

HOW A LEGION WAS ORGAN[...]
Each century had about 80 men. S[...] cohort. The legion was formed fro[...] cohort was made up of the best me[...]

✓ LOOK OUT FOR THESE

□ SWORD AND SCABBARD
The legionary's main weapon was the 'gladius', a short thrusting sword. It wa[s] easy to use in close combat and inflicted terrible gaping wounds.

14

HEADING
The subject matter of each spread is clearly identified by a heading prominently displayed in the top left-hand corner.

DETAILED INFORMATION
From the building of their extraordinary cities and roads to the everyday life of Roman families, the reader is given a wealth of information to help understand the ancient Romans.

ILLUSTRATIONS
High quality, full colour artworks bring the world of the ancient Romans to life. Each spread is packed with visual information.

REFERENCE TAB
Each group of subjects is keyed with a special colour to the contents page of the book so that different sections can be found quickly and easily.

RMY

BRIDGE OF BOATS
Roman armies could cross wide rivers by anchoring boats to the river bed and laying a road across their decks.

WATCHTOWER
Watchtowers lined the empire's borders. Guards used beacon fires to raise the alarm.

LEGIONARIES
Legionaries on the march carried heavy packs, often covering over 30km a day.

CENTURION
A centurion commanded a unit of 80 men called a century. His helmet had a tall crest.

STANDARD BEARER
When attacking, soldiers followed a pole with an emblem on it called a standard. They rallied around it in an emergency.

10 cohorts = legion

800

ned to make a
The larger first

AUXILIARIES
Auxiliaries served as border guards or as specialist soldiers like archers and cavalrymen.

MATTOCK
Each night when on the march, soldiers used tools like these to build an earth rampart around the camp.

MET
protect the
and cheeks
cking
vision.

DISCHARGING DIPLOMA
When legionaries retired they were given land, while auxiliaries gained Roman citizenship. Both were given bronze diplomas.

SILVER INGOT
Roman soldiers often mutinied and they sometimes killed unpopular generals and even emperors. A new emperor would try to win popularity by giving each soldier a gift of money or a valuable silver ingot.

7

THE ROMAN EMPIRE

In 396 BC soldiers from a small Italian city called Rome captured the nearby city of Veii after a long war. Over the next 400 years, the Romans went on to build a vast empire that included many different races of people.

The Romans did not discriminate against people just because they were of a different race or believed in different gods. They encouraged the people they had conquered to adopt Roman customs. They also rewarded loyalty to the empire with citizenship and these people, whether they came from Africa or Syria, Greece or Gaul, thought of themselves as Romans. This is one reason why the Roman empire lasted so long. It was even possible for a man from the provinces to become emperor.

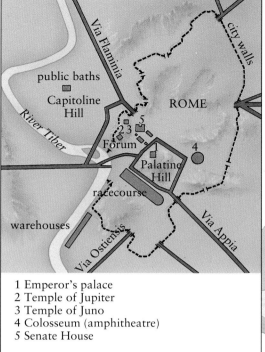

1 Emperor's palace
2 Temple of Jupiter
3 Temple of Juno
4 Colosseum (amphitheatre)
5 Senate House

CITY OF ROME

The first inhabitants of Rome were farmers who lived on the Palatine Hill around 1000 BC. By 50 BC over one million people lived in Rome. The centre was the Forum surrounded by temples, law courts and palaces.

LOOK OUT FOR THESE

FARMER AND WIFE
Wealthy Romans had portraits of themselves carved on their gravestones. This gravestone from the Rhineland shows a farmer and his wife wearing thick woollen cloaks to keep out the cold.

DACIAN
The Dacians were one of the last peoples to be conquered. This nobleman is wearing a Dacian pointed cap.

BAKER
Many Romans, like this successful Italian baker and his wife, had portraits of themselves on the walls of their homes.

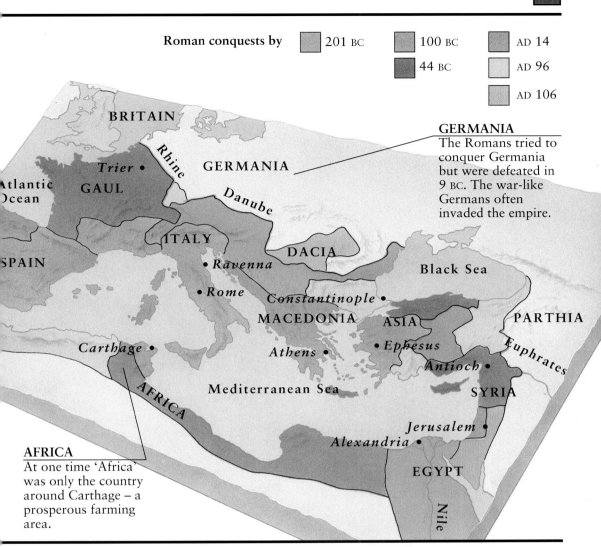

Roman conquests by
- 201 BC
- 100 BC
- 44 BC
- AD 14
- AD 96
- AD 106

BRITAIN

GERMANIA

Atlantic Ocean

GAUL

Trier •

Rhine

Danube

ITALY

• Ravenna

• Rome

SPAIN

DACIA

Black Sea

Constantinople •

MACEDONIA

ASIA

PARTHIA

Carthage •

Athens •

• Ephesus

Antioch •

Euphrates

AFRICA

Mediterranean Sea

SYRIA

Jerusalem •

Alexandria •

EGYPT

Nile

GERMANIA
The Romans tried to conquer Germania but were defeated in 9 BC. The war-like Germans often invaded the empire.

AFRICA
At one time 'Africa' was only the country around Carthage – a prosperous farming area.

GRAVESTONE
Egypt was one of the first areas of the Roman empire to become Christian. This carving shows an Egyptian Christian. Egypt was a rich province but the Romans taxed it very heavily. As a result, Roman rule was most unpopular in Egypt.

SYRIAN FAMILY
Syrians wore exotic clothing. Women wore flowing robes and tall hats. Men wore loose coats and baggy trousers. Most men in the Roman empire were clean shaven but Syrian men liked to grow thick beards. Many Syrians were merchants and traders.

THE ROMAN REPUBLIC

Early Rome was ruled by kings, and was called a monarchy. But in 509 BC the Roman people overthrew the monarchy and founded a republic. Rome was now ruled by officials called magistrates. They were elected each year by a meeting of the Roman people. Experienced politicians called the Senate advised the magistrates.

The Romans were often at war with their neighbours and by 270 BC they had conquered Italy. Carthage, in North Africa, and the Greek states of the east tried to halt Rome's expansion but they were all defeated and by 27 BC the Romans ruled the Mediterranean world.

As Rome grew more powerful, its politicians became corrupt. They gained power through force, not elections, and the republican system broke down.

LICTORS
The consul was escorted by lictors in public. Lictors carried bundles of rods and axes called fasces. These were symbols of the consul's powers.

TOGA
The toga was a semicircular piece of woollen cloth which was wrapped around the body. Only Roman citizens were allowed to wear the toga.

LOOK OUT FOR THESE

RIGHT OF APPEAL
Citizens were protected against wrongful punishment by a right of appeal to the assembly. This could overturn any sentence it thought unjust. This coin shows a prisoner shouting 'provoco' – 'I appeal!'

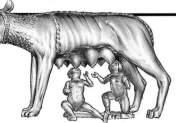

ROMULUS AND REMUS
According to legend, twins called Romulus and Remus were left to die by the River Tiber. They were brought up by a she-wolf. Later they built a city. Romulus killed Remus and named the city Rome after himself.

CONSULS

The consuls were the most senior magistrates. They controlled foreign affairs and commanded the army in wartime. Two consuls were elected each year.

SENATORS

Only men with experience of government were allowed to join the Senate. There were 300 senators and they served for life.

TIMETABLE

1000 BC   Earliest evidence of settlement at Rome
509 BC   Rome becomes a republic
396 BC   Rome begins the conquest of Italy
44 BC   Julius Caesar murdered. Civil war breaks out
27 BC   Augustus becomes the first emperor of Rome
AD 116   The Roman empire reaches its greatest extent
AD 313   Constantine becomes the first Christian Roman emperor
AD 476   The last Roman emperor in the west is deposed

HANNIBAL

The toughest enemy of the republic was Hannibal of Carthage. This painted plate shows his invasion of Italy. In 218 BC Hannibal led an army of 35,000 men and 37 elephants from Spain; he won many battles but was finally defeated.

CICERO

We know what many famous Romans looked like because they had sculptures made of themselves. This bust is of the lawyer Cicero. He was one of Rome's greatest writers.

THE IMPERIAL AGE

After Julius Caesar was murdered in 44 BC, civil war broke out. It was won by Augustus. He made himself commander of the army and could make laws and reject any decision of the Senate. He called himself First Citizen. His successors used the title 'imperator' (commander) from which our word 'emperor' comes. This period of rule by the emperors is known as the imperial age.

Though the emperors were sometimes cruel rulers, they brought peace and prosperity to the empire.

THE EMPEROR
After a successful military campaign the emperor held a parade called a Triumph. A holiday was declared and huge crowds turned out. Afterwards sacrifices were made to thank the gods.

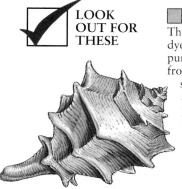

LOOK OUT FOR THESE

MUREX SHELL
The most expensive dye of all was the purple dye that came from the murex sea-snail. Senators were allowed to have a purple stripe on the edge of their togas but only the emperor could dress all in purple.

WINGED VICTORY
The Romans worshipped Victory as a winged goddess who brought success in battle. There were many statues of her, such as this one, on triumphal arches.

ENEMY CHIEFTAIN
Prisoners were dragged through the streets. The leaders were usually executed but the ordinary prisoners were sold as slaves.

CAPTURED ARMS
Heaps of captured arms, treasure and even prisoners were carefully arranged to look like scenes from the battlefield.

AUGUSTUS
This statue shows Augustus as a soldier, the defender of the empire.

COIN
Special coins were sometimes issued to celebrate a new conquest. This coin announces the capture of Egypt by Augustus.

LAUREL LEAVES
Emperors did not wear crowns. Instead, they wore wreaths of laurel as a symbol of their power.

TRIUMPHAL ARCH
Great victories were commemorated by triumphal arches which were decorated with battle scenes. Such arches were built all over the empire and many can still be seen. This one, at Orange in France, celebrated the defeat of a local chieftain who rebelled.

THE ROMAN ARMY

The main reason that the Romans were able to conquer such a large empire was their well-disciplined and highly trained army. The army was an attractive career for poor men. There was the chance of being killed but the wages were good and, if they survived, retired soldiers enjoyed many privileges. The main strength of the army was the legions of infantrymen recruited only from Roman citizens. There were also support troops called auxiliaries.

BRIDGE OF BOATS
Roman armies could cross wide rivers by anchoring boats to the river bed and laying a road across their decks.

WATCHTOWER
Watchtowers lined the empire's borders. Guards used beacon fires to raise the alarm.

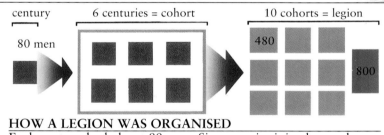

century   6 centuries = cohort   10 cohorts = legion

80 men   480   800

HOW A LEGION WAS ORGANISED
Each century had about 80 men. Six centuries joined to make a cohort. The legion was formed from 10 cohorts. The larger first cohort was made up of the best men.

LOOK OUT FOR THESE

SWORD AND SCABBARD
The legionary's main weapon was the 'gladius', a short thrusting sword. It was easy to use in close combat and inflicted terrible gaping wounds.

HELMET
The helmet was designed to protect the head, neck and cheeks without blocking hearing and vision.

MATTOCK
Each night when on the march, soldiers used tools like these to build an earth rampart around the camp.

LEGIONARIES

Legionaries on the march carried heavy packs, often covering over 30km a day.

CENTURION

A centurion commanded a unit of 80 men called a century. His helmet had a tall crest.

STANDARD BEARER

When attacking, soldiers followed a pole with an emblem on it called a standard. They rallied around it in an emergency.

AUXILIARIES

Auxiliaries served as border guards or as specialist soldiers like archers and cavalrymen.

DISCHARGING DIPLOMA

When legionaries retired they were given land, while auxiliaries gained Roman citizenship. Both were given bronze diplomas.

SILVER INGOT

Roman soldiers often mutinied and they sometimes killed unpopular generals and even emperors. A new emperor would try to win popularity by giving each soldier a gift of money or a valuable silver ingot.

A ROMAN FORT

Most Roman soldiers were stationed in forts close to the borders of the empire. Patrols were sent out from the forts to keep a constant look-out for invaders. Early forts were built of wood but by the 2nd century AD most had been rebuilt in stone. So that soldiers could easily find their way about, each fort had a similar layout. Legionary forts held about 5,000 men. Auxiliary forts, like this one, held only 500-1,000 men.

STABLES
The Roman army used large numbers of horses and ponies as mounts for infantry officers as well as cavalrymen. Mules were used to pull supply carts.

FORT DEFENCES
Fort walls were about 5m high and 3m thick. There were watchtowers at regular intervals along the walls. A deep ditch in front of the walls made it difficult for an enemy to attack.

FORT GATES
There were four well-protected gates so that troops could march out quickly in any direction.

CIVILIAN HOUSES
Innkeepers and shopkeepers settled outside forts hoping to make a living selling drink, food and other goods.

✔ LOOK OUT FOR THESE

▢ GRAVESTONE
This is the gravestone of Romanius, a cavalryman. Soldiers paid part of their wages to a burial club. The club would provide a funeral and gravestone.

▢ STORES LIST
Many soldiers worked as clerks, keeping up-to-date lists of men who were sick or on leave, and of supplies of food and equipment. Instead of using paper, the Romans wrote on sheets of papyrus or, as here, on very thinly cut pieces of wood.

GRANARY
Grain was stored in buildings called granaries, with raised floors to keep out the damp.

PRINCIPIA
The principia was the building which was the headquarters of the fort. It contained offices, archives, a shrine, storerooms and a strongroom where the soldiers' pay was kept.

BATHS
Sparks from the furnaces of the fort's bath house could set fire to the fort, so it was always built outside the walls for safety.

PRAETORIUM
The fort's commander lived with his family in a large, comfortable house called the praetorium.

BARRACKS
Each century had its own barrack block where the soldiers ate and slept. The centurion had a private room. The soldiers slept eight to a room.

MESS TIN
Soldiers had to do their own cooking in ovens which were built into the fort walls. A mess tin was used as a cooking pot and to eat from.

TILE
The army built its own forts and even made its own building materials. This roof tile has the stamp of the 20th Legion on it.

ALTAR
Soldiers liked to worship gods who were believed to bring physical strength and success in battle. This altar was dedicated to Jupiter, the mightiest Roman god, by a cohort of Spanish infantrymen. Mars, Hercules and Mithras were also popular gods.

TOWNS

Roman towns were noisy and crowded places in which to live. Although there were magnificent public buildings most people lived in squalid slums. Fire was a constant hazard and crime was rife. There was no street lighting so most people were afraid to go out after dark. Most towns did have a fire brigade and a police force but neither was very effective. Road accidents and traffic jams were so common that many towns banned wheeled vehicles from the streets in daytime.

Despite all this, the Romans thought that towns were the best places to live. They had the things that the Romans thought were very important in life: theatres, amphitheatres, racecourses, hot baths, taverns and take-away food shops.

AMPHITHEATRE
This was used for bloodthirsty shows like gladiator fights.

THEATRE
Audiences at the theatre sat in a semicircle facing the stage.

TEMPLE
Roman temple architecture closely copied Greek styles. Temples were usually built on a raised platform.

LOOK OUT FOR THESE

PILLAR CAPITALS
The tops of pillars (called capitals) were richly carved. The two main types used by the Romans were the Corinthian (left) and Ionic (right) styles. The Romans copied these styles from the Greeks.

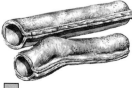

LEAD PIPES
Lead was moulded around wooden rods to make water pipes. As lead was poisonous they only used it where they could not use clay.

PUBLIC FOUNTAIN
Only very rich people could afford to have water piped directly to their houses. Everyone else used water from the public fountains.

FORUM
The forum was the town's main meeting place and market square. The covered sides contained shops and offices.

BATHS
Every town had at least one public bath house, large towns usually had several. Baths were popular social centres.

AQUEDUCT
Aqueducts brought supplies of clean drinking water to the town.

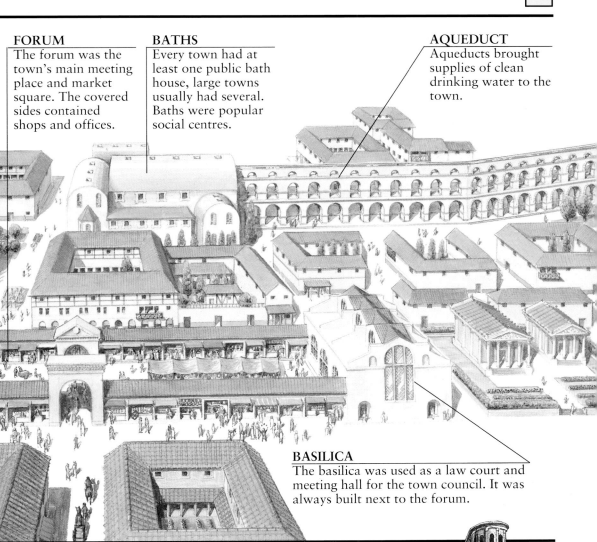

BASILICA
The basilica was used as a law court and meeting hall for the town council. It was always built next to the forum.

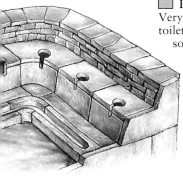

LATRINES
Very few people had toilets in their houses, so multi-seater public latrines had to be built around the town. The latrines were connected to the town's underground sewers.

CITY GATES
Many Roman cities had walls to protect them from attack. However, strong walls and impressive looking gatehouses, like this one at Trier in Germany, were also seen as a sign of the city's importance.

BUILDING TECHNOLOGY

The Romans were skilful builders. Roman buildings were very strong and many are still standing today. Most Roman buildings were built of bricks and concrete. Stone was expensive so it was often used just to decorate buildings. Roman builders were the first to become expert at using concrete and building arches. The Romans also invented the dome. Because of these skills their buildings could be very spacious, with high roofs and big windows.

Some of the best builders and surveyors were in the army. In peacetime the army helped to plan and build whole towns. Town councils also owned slaves who were used as labourers on building sites.

WINDOWS
Glass windows were very expensive. Only important buildings had them.

ROMAN WALL
Two low brick or stone walls were built with a space in-between. Then the space was filled with concrete. Another layer could be built on top after the concrete had dried.

LOOK OUT FOR THESE

ROOF TILES
Roof tiles were moulded out of clay then baked in a kiln. The tiles were stamped with the name of the factory that made them.

ARCHITECTS' AND MASONS' TOOLS
The tools shown here are a folding ruler, dividers, a set square and a plumb line. A plumb line was used to check that walls were straight. The ruler measures a Roman foot (296mm).

CONCRETE

Concrete was made out of lime, sand and small stones. Concrete was very useful for building roofs. It weighed less than stone and could not catch fire like wood. It was also cheap to make.

ROOF BUILDING

A temporary wooden arch was built first. A layer of bricks was laid on top of the arch. A layer of concrete was then poured over the bricks.

CRANE

Cranes lifted heavy loads. They were operated by slaves walking inside a treadmill.

TOOLS

This carpenter's hammer and bricklayer's trowel are almost identical to ones that you might find on a modern building site.

INSCRIPTION

Inscriptions are found on many Roman buildings. They explain when they were built and who built them. This inscription comes from a theatre at Leptis Magna, Africa.

ROADS AND TRAVEL

The Roman empire had an excellent system of roads. Most roads were built by the army. This is because the roads were built mainly to allow soldiers to travel quickly in wartime. However, they also benefited trade. The roads made it easier for merchants to carry their goods around the empire.

Sometimes well-off people went on sightseeing trips but most people did not travel unless they had to. They lived in the same town or village all their lives and rarely left it. Some Roman roads are still used today. They are easy to spot on a map because they often run for long distances in very straight lines.

SURVEYING

The route was surveyed using a groma. This was difficult to use. It had to be kept perfectly level and even a breeze could cause problems. The route was marked out with stakes.

LOOK OUT FOR THESE

MILESTONES

A Roman mile was about 1,460m long. Each mile along a road was marked off by a stone. They were like modern roadsigns. They told the traveller how far he had to go to reach the next town.

ROAD MAP

This is a small part of a Roman road map. The map shows the roads and the distances between the towns and cities of the empire. Mountains, rivers and seas are also shown. Maps helped travellers plan their journeys and work out how long they would take.

BRIDGE BUILDING

The Romans built strong arched bridges using stone and concrete. This bridge in Spain is still in use today, more than 1,800 years later. It is over 45m high.

PAVING SLABS

The road was paved with hard-wearing stone slabs. The middle of the road was made higher than the sides so rain would drain off.

LAYERS OF PEBBLES AND GRAVEL

A layer of pebbles and gravel was rammed down to form a hard surface.

DIGGING

The Romans dug a trench 1m deep and 7m wide. Drainage ditches were also dug alongside the road.

FOUNDATIONS

The trench was covered with sand and large stones. These were packed tightly to make strong foundations.

■ SLIP-ON SHOE

Horses wore iron shoes to protect their hoofs when travelling on roads. The shoes were held on with rope.

■ STAGE COACH

The Roman empire had an official postal service. Stage coaches carried mail and government officials all over the empire. Travel was slow. Coaches travelled only 35-50km a day and they were bumpy and uncomfortable to ride in.

Farming and the Countryside

Over 90 per cent of the people of the Roman empire lived in the countryside. Many were slaves who worked on the estates of rich landowners. Some were labourers who found work wherever they could. Others were tenant farmers (they paid rent for their land). Nearly all of them were poor. The slaves had the hardest lives of all and were treated harshly.

Country life was governed by the seasons. This picture shows some autumn activities on an Italian farm.

VINEYARD

Vines were grown to produce grapes for eating and making wine. Wine was made by pouring grape juice into large jars and leaving it to ferment. The harvest was in October.

SHEEP SHEARING

Wool was the most important textile in Roman times. The sheep were sheared in April, before the weather got too hot. Sheep were also kept for meat and milk.

LOOK OUT FOR THESE

GRAIN MEASURE

Tenant farmers often paid rent and taxes in grain rather than money. This bronze grain measure was used by tax collectors.

PLOUGHS

Two kinds of plough were used. The one in the foreground, called an ard, could only work light soils.

TOOLS

Farm workers used iron tools. These are sheep shears, a sickle and a hoe for weeding.

PLOUGHING

The fields were ploughed before wheat and barley were sown in November. Oxen were used to draw ploughs and wagons.

VILLA

The villa was the centre of a large estate. There was a comfortable house for the owner and his family and a farmyard with barns, stables and workshops.

OLIVE TREES

Olives were an important crop in the Mediterranean. They were crushed to make olive oil. This was used for cooking and as fuel for oil lamps.

SHEEP

Lambs in Italy were born in November so they could grow up in the mild winter.

HARVESTING MACHINES

Crops were usually harvested by hand using a sickle, but some large farms used harvesting machines like this one.

LABOURER

This bronze model from Gaul shows a farm labourer in winter clothes. He is wearing a short hooded cloak, a tunic and leggings. With no waterproof coats or boots, outdoor work in winter was wet and cold. Farm labourers were poorly paid.

TRADE AND SHIPS

Trade was very important to the Roman empire. Big cities like Rome had to import large amounts of food from all over the empire. Luxury goods came from further away. Silk came on camel caravans from China. Ships brought spices, jewels and perfumes from India. Transporting goods on land was expensive so most trade went by sea. Roman merchant ships were strong and seaworthy but very slow. Sailing was dangerous and ships stayed in port from November to March to avoid winter storms.

BARGE
Flat-bottomed barges were used to transport goods on rivers to seaports.

SAILS
Roman merchant ships were driven by a single large square sail. A smaller sail at the front was used to help steer the ship.

GALLEY
The Roman navy used galleys to patrol the sea against pirates. Oarsmen were highly trained professional sailors.

LOOK OUT FOR THESE

■ **BARREL**
The barrel was invented by the Celts of northern Europe. The Romans copied the idea and used barrels to transport beer and wine.

■ **AMBER**
Amber is a valuable yellow-coloured resin. German tribesmen collected amber from around the Baltic Sea and sold it to Roman traders. Amber can be carved easily into figurines. The Romans also believed that it had magical and medical properties.

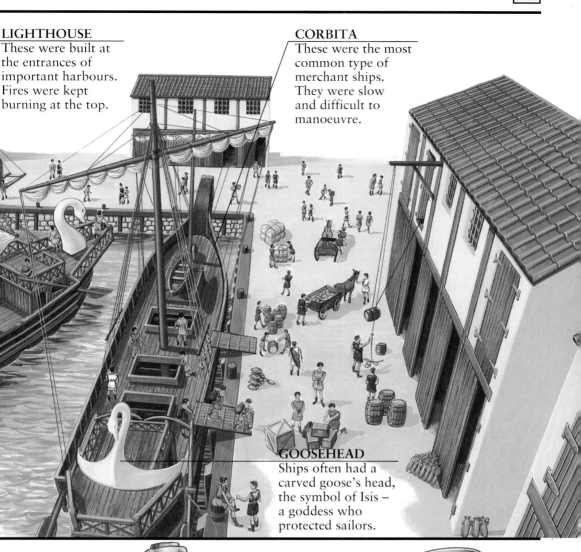

LIGHTHOUSE
These were built at the entrances of important harbours. Fires were kept burning at the top.

CORBITA
These were the most common type of merchant ships. They were slow and difficult to manoeuvre.

GOOSEHEAD
Ships often had a carved goose's head, the symbol of Isis – a goddess who protected sailors.

DOCKERS' TOOLS
These iron tools were used for handling cargo and opening packing crates.

AMPHORAE
Amphorae were tall clay jars with pointed bases. They were used as containers for liquids such as wine, olive oil and garum (fish paste). Millions of amphorae were made and most of them were thrown away after being used just once.

POTTERY
Factories making high quality pottery traded their goods all over the empire. This pottery was made in Gaul.

THE TOWN HOUSE

Most townspeople lived in multistorey apartment blocks. Richer people lived in the lower storeys. These were built of brick and had large comfortable rooms. Poorer people lived in the higher storeys. These were built of wood and the rooms were small and draughty. None of the apartments had kitchens, water or toilets. The ground floors were rented out as shops. Only rich people owned their own homes. This picture shows the kind of house that a rich Italian family might have lived in.

SHOP
Shopkeepers often rented out the front rooms and lived in small rooms above the shop.

MOSAIC
Mosaics are patterns or pictures made out of tiny squares of coloured pottery. Laying mosaics was a very skilled job. Mosaics were laid on the floors of houses and public buildings.

ATRIUM
This was the central courtyard. A hole in the roof let in light, and a basin collected rainwater.

LOOK OUT FOR THESE

SHRINE
The Romans believed that the family's fortune was governed by household spirits. The Lares guarded the family while the Penates watched over the food. Every house had a shrine dedicated to these spirits.

FLOWERS
The Romans' favourite flower was the rose. Private gardens were planted with rows of rose bushes. The Romans grew many other flowers such as marigolds, irises and delphiniums. Peonies were popular as people thought they could be used as a medicine.

WORKROOMS

Slaves' quarters and workrooms were at the back of the house.

WINDOW

Windows were very small to stop burglars.

PERISTYLE

The peristyle was an open courtyard with a covered walk around the edges. The peristyle was decorated with flower beds, fountains and statues.

TABLINIUM

The tablinium was the main living room of the house. It was usually built between the atrium and the peristyle. Guests were entertained there.

BEDROOM

Bedrooms were small and simply furnished.

SHOES

Outdoors, Romans wore leather sandals or boots. At home they usually went barefoot or wore light slippers.

PORTABLE BRAZIER

Roman houses did not have fireplaces or chimneys. Rooms were heated with portable braziers made of bronze. Charcoal was burned on the braziers because it gave off less smoke than wood.

OIL LAMP

Candles and oil lamps were used for indoor lighting. Oil lamps were made of pottery or bronze. They burned olive oil. Candles were luxury items.

FAMILY LIFE

Roman families were small. Parents usually had three children or less. Children were expected to grow up quickly. Children in poor families had to start work as young as five or six. Richer children did little but play until they were seven. Boys then started school. Most left at 11 to learn the family business. Boys were considered to be adults at 14. Girls were educated at home. They were taught how to run a household by their mothers. Most girls were engaged by 12 and married by 14.

Parents were affectionate towards their children but they expected to be obeyed. Marriages often ended in divorce. If this happened, the children always stayed with the father. The Romans believed that age brought wisdom. Because of this, they respected aged relatives.

THE SON
Romans preferred sons to daughters because only sons could carry on the family name. If a couple was childless or only had daughters, they would adopt a son.

THE FATHER
Fathers had the right to whip or jail their sons. They could even sell them as slaves. Few fathers were that cruel but they were always strict.

LOOK OUT FOR THESE

MODEL OF A BABY
Soon after birth the baby was wrapped tightly in bands of linen swaddling clothes. A baby's chances of surviving to adulthood were poor. Around half would die before the age of five.

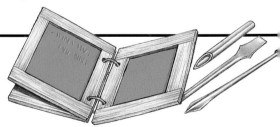

TABLET AND STYLUS
Children learned to write using wooden tablets covered with wax. The letters were formed in the wax using a metal stylus. The pointed end was used for writing. The blunt end was used to smooth the wax.

SLAVES

Household slaves were often well treated. Many were freed as a reward for good service.

WET NURSE

The wet nurse was a slave who looked after children. She washed, dressed and fed them, played with them and helped in their education. Children often only saw their parents at the evening meal.

THE MOTHER

With slaves looking after her children, the mother could concentrate on managing the household.

TOYS

Roman boys liked to play with marbles. Girls played with rag dolls. Before marrying, girls gave up their dolls to show they were now adults.

SLAVE'S COLLAR AND 'DOG TAG'

Slaves who were thought likely to run away were treated like dogs. They had to wear metal collars or name plates. These gave the name and address of the slave's owner. If they were caught, they were sent straight back home and punished.

RINGS

On becoming engaged a couple exchanged rings. Late June was a popular time for weddings. It was thought to be a lucky time of year.

FOOD AND DRINK

The Romans ate three meals a day. Breakfast was bread and fruit. At midday they ate a light lunch of bread, cheese, cold fish, meat and vegetables. The main meal of the day was a three-course dinner served in the evening. Not all Romans ate as well as this in the evening.

Most people lived in apartments which did not have kitchens. They either had to eat cold meals or buy hot food from the many take-away food shops. The poorest Romans had a very bad diet. They were given hand-outs of grain from the government which they made into porridge.

BUTCHER'S SHOP
Roman shops were small and sold a limited range of products. This butcher sells only pork, the Romans' favourite meat. The butcher would advertise his shop by hanging a model of a leg of pork on the wall outside.

 **LOOK OUT FOR THESE**

☐ **STRAINER**
Food in Roman times was not as pure as the food we eat today. Wine usually contained grape pips and bits of stalk. Before it could be drunk, wine was filtered through a strainer. This was a large metal spoon with small holes in it.

☐ **MORTAR AND PESTLE**
Every kitchen had a mortar and pestle. They were used for grinding herbs and spices to be used when making sauces.

TRICLINIUM

The dining room of the house was called the triclinium. Diners reclined on three couches which were arranged around a low dining table.

KITCHEN

Food was cooked over a brick oven. It was either boiled in a pot or roasted on a griddle over the flames. Cooking was hard work and the evening meal could take all day to prepare. Cooks were valued household slaves.

EVENING MEAL

The main meal had three courses: a starter of eggs, seafood or snails, a main course of roast or boiled meat and a last course of sweets and fruit.

◻ GLASS FLAGON

After straining, wine was poured into fine glass flagons. Glass vessels like this were made by blowing a blob of molten glass into a mould. Glass was very expensive and broken bottles were collected and recycled, just as they are today.

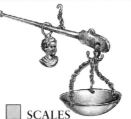

◻ SCALES

Shopkeepers used scales like these to weigh food. The Romans measured weight in pounds and ounces.

◻ BREAD

Bread was sold while still hot from the oven. The dough was shaped so that the finished loaf could easily be divided up.

THE PUBLIC BATHS

Romans enjoyed going to the baths. The baths were cheap to enter so both rich and poor could afford to go often. Those who could spare the time went every day. Men and women had separate rooms in the baths as mixed bathing was not allowed.

People did not go to the baths just to get clean. The baths were a place to meet friends and gossip, gamble or play games. You could have a massage or go for a swim. Some baths had restaurants and even libraries.

HOT ROOM
The heat and steam made bathers sweat, getting rid of dirt in the pores of their skin.

STEAM BATH
Furnaces boiled pools of water to fill the hot room with steam.

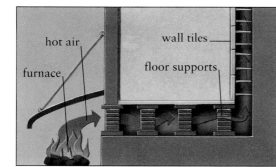

hot air

furnace

wall tiles

floor supports

HYPOCAUST
A hypocaust was a heating system in which hot air from a furnace circulated under the floor and inside flues built into the walls, warming the room.

LOOK OUT FOR THESE

▦ STRIGIL AND OIL FLASK
The Romans did not use soap to keep clean. Instead, they poured olive oil onto their bodies. Then the oil, along with any dirt on the skin, was scraped off with a strigil. This was made of wood or metal.

▦ TOOTHPICKS
After a meal people carefully removed any food from their teeth with toothpicks. These toothpicks are made of silver. Romans kept their teeth white by rinsing with a mouthwash.

WARM ROOM

Before entering the hot room bathers went to the warm room to get used to the heat.

COLD ROOM

Bathers went to the cold room last of all. Here they had a quick dip in a pool of cold water to give the skin a final rinse.

EXERCISE AND GAMING AREA

Before going home bathers liked to sunbathe and chat with their friends. Some also did athletic exercises.

SPONGE

Instead of toilet paper, the Romans used sponges on sticks. After use, the sponge was washed and dried so that it could be used again.

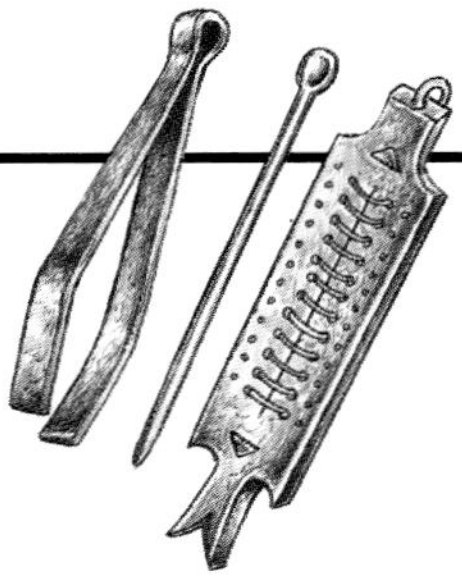

MANICURE SET

This pocket sized manicure set includes a pair of tweezers, a tiny spoon for scooping out ear wax and a nail file.

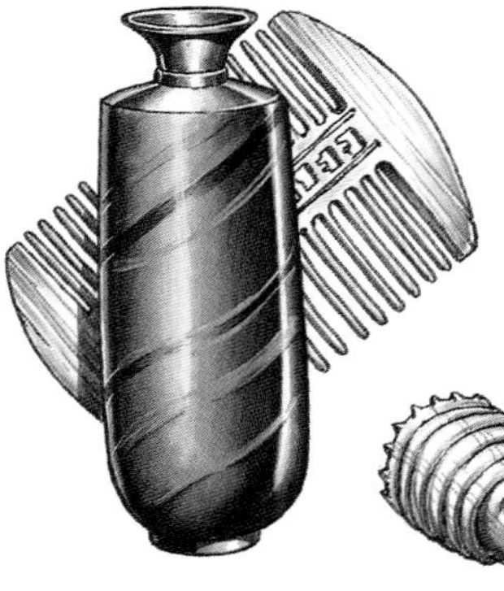

TOILETRIES

Roman women made themselves look and smell beautiful with make-up and perfume. However, they paid most attention to their hair. Pictured here are a polished stone perfume bottle and a bone comb and hairpin.

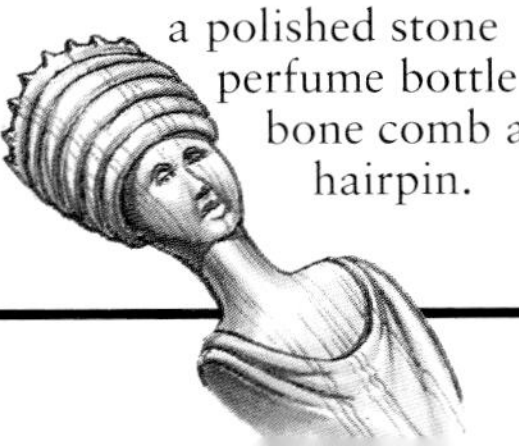

ENTERTAINMENTS

Most entertainments in the Roman empire were free. Events were paid for by rich and ambitious men. By putting on a lavish show they hoped to gain popularity and improve their chances of winning elections for positions in politics.

Though it was free to enter, people were not allowed to sit anywhere they liked in the arena or theatre. Front seats were reserved for the rich. Poorer people sat behind and slaves had to sit right at the back.

Musical theatre and concerts were popular but the best attended events were violent ones like chariot races and gladiator shows. The main event at gladiator shows was a fight between men armed with different kinds of weapons.

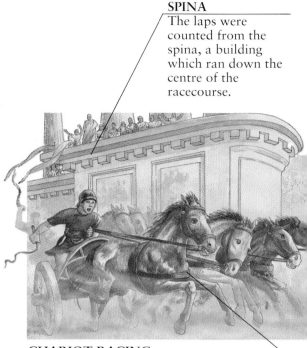

SPINA
The laps were counted from the spina, a building which ran down the centre of the racecourse.

CHARIOT RACING
Chariots were usually drawn by four horses. Races lasted for seven laps, with four chariots in each race. Each team of charioteers had its own supporters. They often fought each other and it was not unusual for dozens of people to be killed. Chariot races were the most popular form of entertainment.

LOOK OUT FOR THESE

BOARD GAME
The Romans liked to play board games with counters and dice. Unfortunately, no rule books have survived so we do not know how the games were played.

ACTOR'S MASK
All actors wore masks which had exaggerated expressions. This was to help the audience, because many people had to sit a long way from the stage. This is the mask of a tragic character.

RETIARIUS

The retiarius was a gladiator armed with a net and trident. He would entangle his opponent in the net before spearing him.

THEATRE

Two plays were shown at a theatrical event. The first was a tragedy. There were dramatic effects and music. The tragedy was supposed to make everyone sad, so the second play was a comedy.

MURMILLO

The murmillo was a heavily armoured gladiator. He could be a dangerous opponent. His only weakness was that his helmet obstructed his vision.

HELMET

This richly decorated bronze helmet probably belonged to a champion gladiator. The grille at the front protected the face.

GLASS TROPHY

This glass trophy was made to celebrate a victory by a charioteer called Crescens.

MOSAIC

This mosaic shows two men bringing in a deer after a successful hunt. Much of the countryside was still wild and there was a lot of wildlife. Hunting deer and wild boar was a popular pastime for country people.

RELIGION

There were many Roman gods. Each watched over a different activity of daily life. The Romans were afraid of their gods. The gods could easily be made angry and if that happened, all sorts of disasters might follow. Regular sacrifices had to be made to keep the gods happy. No important decision, like declaring war, would be taken unless the Romans were sure that the gods would approve.

The Romans believed in life after death. They thought that a dead person's spirit was ferried across an underground river called the Styx, to Hades – the land of the dead. Here the spirits were judged. The good went to heaven, the bad to hell. At funerals a coin was placed under the dead person's tongue. This was to pay the ferry fare to Hades.

ALTAR
Altars were set up outside temples. The priest placed the offerings mixed with incense and holy oil on the altar. These were all burned so that the smoke could take the offerings to the god.

LOOK OUT FOR THESE

CREMATION URN
The Romans either buried their dead or cremated them. After cremation, the ashes were put in an urn for burial. Cremation urns came in all shapes and could be made of pottery, metal or even glass. This 'face urn' is from Roman Britain.

JUPITER
Jupiter was the ruler of the Roman gods. He was known as Best and Greatest. Jupiter stood for good faith, honour and justice. When he was angry Jupiter hurled thunderbolts and caused storms. His wife was Juno, the goddess who protected women.

MUSIC

Solemn music was performed before the sacrifice. At the kill the priest called for silence.

PRIEST

The priest had to make sure that the sacrifice was performed correctly. Any mistake would mean that the sacrifice would not be accepted by the god.

SACRED KNIFE

The animals were first knocked to the ground with an axe. Then their throats were cut with a sacred knife.

ANIMALS

A pig, sheep and bull were sacrificed at important ceremonies.

MARS

Mars was the god of war and country life. He was the guardian of Rome and would avenge any wrong.

MINERVA

Minerva, the goddess of wisdom, watched over writers, doctors, teachers, artists and craftsmen.

CHARM

People who were sick prayed to the gods for a cure. People gave models of the sick or injured part of the body to the god to show their gratitude if they were cured.

THE LATE ROMAN EMPIRE

In the 3rd century AD the empire suffered so many invasions that it almost collapsed. It was saved by a series of soldier-emperors who restored the empire's defences. The rule of these emperors was harsh. Taxes were high to pay for the defences and tax collectors were ruthless.

Christians had been persecuted in the early empire. But in AD 313 the emperor Constantine became a Christian. He built many churches and helped spread the religion. Within 100 years most people in the empire were Christians.

BUREAUCRATS
Officials were needed to collect taxes and keep records of spending.

WALLS OF CONSTANTINOPLE
The threat of invasion meant that cities were given strong defences. These mighty walls were built around Constantinople.

LOOK OUT FOR THESE

SARCOPHAGUS
A sarcophagus was a stone or marble tomb. It was often richly decorated. The symbol of the cross on the side of this one's lid tells us that it was used for a Christian burial.

SILVER VOTIVE PLAQUE
This plaque carries the 'chi-rho' sign. It stood for Kristos, the Greek name for Christ. Gifts of these plaques were made to the church.

FLASK
Many Christians liked to visit the shrines of famous saints. They took flasks filled with holy oil home with them as souvenirs.

CLOTHING
The toga was no longer fashionable. Romans now wore rich and colourful clothes.

EMPEROR
The emperor was a figure of awesome majesty. The Christian emperors claimed to rule the empire as Christ's deputies.

SILVER SPOONS
Christians gave presents to people when they were baptised. One of the most popular baptismal presents was a set of silver spoons. Baptism was an important ceremony. It was believed to bring the soul into closer union with Christ.

IVORY PLAQUE
Officials announced their promotion to new posts with these carved ivory plaques. This official has just been made a consul. Consuls were still important men but they were not as powerful as they had been in the republic.

THE END OF THE ROMAN EMPIRE

In the 5th century AD the Roman empire again came under attack from outside. This time there were no soldier-emperors to save it. By now the emperors had become weak and powerless figures. They were dominated by their officials and generals. The invaders were Germanic barbarian tribesmen. They did not invade because they wanted to destroy the Roman empire. They wanted to live in it and share in its wealth.

The Romans gave the barbarians lands in which to settle. In return the barbarians agreed to help defend the empire. This worked for a time. But the barbarians began to take more land. By AD 476 they had taken over all of the western half of the empire. The eastern half survived for another 1,000 years. It became known as the Byzantine empire.

BARBARIANS

The barbarians who invaded the empire brought their families with them. They travelled in covered wagons or on foot. In return for being given land to farm, many of the men joined the Roman army.

LOOK OUT FOR THESE

HELMET
Most barbarian warriors could not afford helmets or armour. This beautifully decorated helmet probably belonged to a king. He would only have worn it on special occasions, such as parades. It was far too valuable to wear in a real battle.

JEWELLERY
Both barbarian men and women wore jewellery. Most jewellery served a practical purpose. Bow-brooches like this were used to fasten cloaks. Decorated belt-buckles were also popular. The finest jewellery was made of decorated gold.

CHIEFTAIN

The power of a barbarian chieftain depended on his skill in battle. Only a leader who was successful in winning wealth and land for his people could expect them to be loyal to him.

LANDOWNER

In return for giving some of his land to the barbarians, the government would let the landowner off some of his taxes. He also hoped the barbarians would protect his estates.

ARMY OFFICER

Roman uniforms and armour had changed a lot since early Imperial times.

CREMATION JAR

The barbarians cremated their dead. Then they buried the ashes in earthenware jars like this.

 DRINKING HORN

Drinking horns could not stand up so the beer or wine in them was supposed to be swallowed in one go.

WEAPONS

The barbarians' favourite weapon was the sword. Particularly fine swords even had their own names. Swords were too expensive for most barbarians to afford. Most fought with a spear, a dagger and a wooden shield.

GLOSSARY

Words in SMALL CAPITAL letters indicate a cross-reference.

altar A stone table on which sacrifices were offered to the gods.

amphitheatre A circular building where GLADIATOR fights took place.

archive A room where documents are stored.

Augustus The first EMPEROR of Rome. He ruled 27 BC-AD 14. He added Egypt and many other territories to the Roman empire.

auxiliary A soldier who was recruited from the PROVINCES of the Roman empire. Auxiliaries served as support troops and were not as well paid as soldiers in the LEGIONS.

Baltic Sea A sea in northern Europe.

barbarian A word used by the Romans to describe the less civilized peoples who lived outside their empire.

barracks A building used to house soldiers.

beacon A signal fire used to give warning of an invasion.

brazier A portable heater used for burning CHARCOAL.

bureaucrat A government official.

Carthage A rich and powerful trading city in North Africa. Rome and Carthage were bitter enemies.

cavalryman A soldier who fights on horseback.

Celts An important nation of northern Europe. They were the ancestors of the modern Welsh, Irish and Scottish.

charcoal A black coal-like fuel made by heating wood.

Cicero A famous Roman lawyer and writer who lived 106-43 BC.

citizen Two classes of people lived in the Roman empire: citizens and non-citizens. Citizens had more rights than non-citizens and could vote in elections.

cohort An army unit of 400 soldiers.

Colosseum A famous AMPHITHEATRE in Rome. It could seat as many as 75,000 people.

Constantine The first Roman emperor to become a Christian. He ruled AD 306-337.

Constantinople A great city founded by CONSTANTINE. It became the capital of the eastern half of the Roman empire. It is now called Istanbul.

consul The most senior government officer in the Roman REPUBLIC. Two were elected each year. They lost power under the EMPERORS.

cremation Burning a dead body to ash before burial.

dictator A ruler who holds supreme power. The Romans appointed dictators to rule during emergencies. They were supposed to retire after one year.

docker A person who works loading or unloading ships.

emperor A king-like ruler who held supreme power in the Roman state.

forum The main market and meeting place.

Gaul A PROVINCE which covered modern France and Belgium.

Germania A region which included modern Germany and eastern Europe. It was inhabited by war-like tribes.

gladiator A slave specially trained to fight in the AMPHITHEATRE.

groma An instrument used by surveyors to measure straight lines and right angles.

Hercules A legendary hero of great strength. He became a god after his death.

infantryman A soldier who fights on foot.

Isis An Egyptian goddess who was worshipped by sailors.

ivory A hard white material that comes from elephants' tusks.

Julius Caesar A Roman general who conquered GAUL. He was murdered by the Senate after making himself DICTATOR for life in 44 BC.

Juno The wife of JUPITER, the Romans' chief god.

Jupiter The Romans' chief god. He ruled over all the other gods.

legion The main fighting unit of the Roman army. Each legion contained about 4,500 soldiers.

Leptis Magna An important port in North Africa.

Mars The Roman god of war.

Mason A craftsman trained to shape stones for building.

Mithras A warrior god who was worshipped by many Roman soldiers.

monarchy A form of government where the highest authority is held by a king or queen.

papyrus A reed which was used to make paper.

Parthia A powerful kingdom on the eastern border of the Roman empire.

province One of the regions of the Roman empire outside Italy (e.g. GAUL).

republic A form of government where supreme power is held by officers elected by the people.

sculpture The art of making figures by carving stone or wood.

shrine A room or container where sacred objects were kept or worshipped.

slave A person who is owned by another. Slaves had to do what their owners told them and they could not own property.

stylus A pointed tool which was used for writing on wax tablets.

surveyor A person who is trained to mark out on the ground where new roads or buildings are to be built.

INDEX